For Tom and Benji
(whose favourite question is 'why?')
- L.K.

For Eiji, Isla
and Alyssa.
- J.L.

For Juan Pablo :)
- N.R-C.

A TEMPLAR BOOK

First published in the UK in 2025 by Templar Books,
an imprint of Bonnier Books UK
5th Floor, HYLO, 103–105 Bunhill Row,
London, EC1Y 8LZ
Owned by Bonnier Books
Sveavägen 56, Stockholm, Sweden
www.bonnierbooks.co.uk

Text copyright © 2025 by Jonathan Litton and Laura Knowles
Illustration copyright © 2025 by Natalia Rojas Castro
Design copyright © 2025 by Templar Books

1 3 5 7 9 10 8 6 4 2

All rights reserved

ISBN 978-1-78741-506-5

This book was typeset in
LosLana Niu Pro and PT Sans
The illustrations were created digitally

Written by Jonathan Litton and Laura Knowles
Edited by Rachael Roberts and Sophie Hallam
Designed by Jeni Child
Production by Neil Randles

Printed in Malaysia

FLAGS

Written by
**JONATHAN LITTON
& LAURA KNOWLES**

Illustrated by
**NATALIA
ROJAS CASTRO**

templar
books

CONTENTS

The History of Flags 8
Anatomy of a Flag 10

EUROPE 12
Three Flags in One 14
From Heavens Above 16
A Flag for a Fleet 18
The Famous Tricolore 20
Uniting a Nation 22

What Do Flag Colours Mean? 24

ASIA 26
Land of the Rising Sun 28
A Five-Star Flag 30
Gandhi's Flag 32
Script and Sword 34
Doing Things Differently 36
Land of the Thunder Dragon 37

Flags of Faith 38

THE AMERICAS 40
The Star-Spangled Banner 42
Order and Progress 44
The Maple Leaf.................................. 46
One Nation, Two Flags 48
The Purple Parrot 50

The Sun and Moon 52

AFRICA 54
Forever Free 56
Land of Warriors 58
A Symbol of Freedom....................... 60
A Flag for a Fresh Start 62

A Flag Menagerie 64

OCEANIA 66
The Southern Cross 68
A Colourful Country 70
The Boar's Tusk Flag 72

Fun Flag Oddities 74

Flag Index 76
Glossary.. 77

Use the index to find a particular flag or country!

THE FABRIC OF NATIONS

Every country in the world has a national flag. One country has two, and most countries have other flags as well – naval flags, presidential flags and regional flags, to name but a few. But no flag captures an identity as well as a national flag. National flags represent the histories, ambitions, landscapes and cultures of nations – all woven into the fabric of fluttering cloth.

People have fought for flags and died for flags. Some have been flying for centuries, whereas others are much newer. Some are very simple, while others are incredibly detailed, and they often come in families, just like the countries they represent. Flags hold on to history, like stories told in tapestries.

So get ready to explore, and unfurl, the remarkable world of flags, from the USA's stars and stripes to China's five-star red flag, from Japan's round sun to Bhutan's thunder dragon, from Ethiopia's proud use of yellow, green and red to the rare sight of purple on the flag of Dominica, from an Egyptian eagle to a Papua New Guinean bird of paradise, and so much more!

THE HISTORY OF FLAGS

Around the world, since early civilisation, people of all cultures have used arrangements of colours and shapes to represent regions, tribes, families, religions and philosophies. Beads, tattoos, clothes, hats and jewellery are all examples of such symbols, but few are as recognisable as a flag.

Flags large and small have been used to identify people, their country or affiliation, clearly and at a distance. It could even be a matter of life or death, such as on the battlefield or out at sea, to flag whether you were a friend or enemy.

The Shahdad Standard, thought to be from 2400 BCE, is a Middle Eastern banner featuring an intricate design displayed on a sheet of bronze, attached to a long, metal pole.

THE WORLD BEFORE FLAGS

Early societies in Europe, Asia, the Middle East and Africa all have examples of **vexilloids** – flag-like objects – with some even thought to be around 3,000 years old. The ancient Egyptians carried 'standards' to battles: solid objects – commonly representing a sacred animal – attached to the top of a pole. Another design often seen was a semi-circular fan.

CUT FROM CLOTH

Around the 11th century BCE, people across the Asian continent started using silk and cloth for their flags. In China, the Zhou Dynasty army would carry white banners into battle. This trend of fabric banners would catch on, and it became particularly popular with the Roman Empire and its legions. In India, intricate carvings were replicated onto triangular cloth pennants.

GETTING PERSONAL

In Europe, during the **Middle Ages**, important families began to use personalised symbols not only on shields and signs but also on cloth banners, both for the battlefield and for peaceful displays.

Other medieval flags included the Vikings' raven banner and green flags in the early days of Islam.

SEE US AT SEA

During the **Age of Sail** (16th–19th century), the world opened up and both trade and war ships needed to know who they were sharing the waters with. Flags were solidified as symbols of identity and affiliation, and the national flag was born.

LIVING HISTORY

As nations developed over time, so too did flags. Some symbols and traditions have remained since their conception. In Europe, complicated **coats of arms** and intricate symbols were simplified into two- and three-coloured flags for easy recognition.

Flags continue to change to this very day. In December 2023, Kyrgyzstan redesigned the sun symbol that sits in its flag's centre. Some people supported this, while others were against it, and maybe it will change once again. Maybe many flags will change in your lifetime, their meanings evolving with new events we're yet to see. The timeline of changes in flags and their meanings shows us that history is living and breathing.

ANATOMY OF A FLAG

If you've ever watched the parade at an opening ceremony of the Olympic Games, you'll have spotted each team proudly waving their country's flag. Each flag is unique, but they also share many similar features, just like humans do. Here are the main parts that make up a flag:

Hoist side – the side of the flag next to the flagpole

Canton – a quarter of a flag, almost always used to describe the upper corner on the hoist side

Charge – a symbol appearing in the field of a flag

Field – the background of the flag, sometimes also called the ground

Fly side – the side of the flag furthest from the flagpole

Flagpole

FLAG PATTERNS

Although every country's flag is different, there are some basic patterns that are used often. Here are the main ones you will come across – see if you can spot them as you read the book.

- Border
- Canton
- Quarterly (or Quadrisection)
- Greek Cross
- Symmetric Cross
- Nordic Cross
- Pales
- Fesses
- Bends
- Chevron
- Pall
- Saltire

BIG, BOLD STRIPES

A flag with a two-colour background is called a bicolour ('bi' means two). The colours could be split horizontally, vertically or diagonally. If a flag has three stripes, it's called a triband. Tribands with three different colours are called tricolours.

↑ Nigeria's triband flag contains only two colours: green for natural wealth and white for unity and peace.

↑ Lithuania's bright tricolour was banned while the country was part of the **Soviet Union**.

↑ Ukraine's flag is a bicolour. The band of blue represents the sky and the yellow represents wheat, a crop it is famous for.

Poland

Switzerland

KEEPING THINGS IN PROPORTION

Although almost all flags are rectangular, some are narrow, while others are closer to a square. These differences are known as a flag's ratio. The most common ratio is 2:3, meaning the flag is one-and-a-half times as wide as it is tall. Almost half of all national flags use this ratio. The next most common ratio is 1:2, used by more than a quarter of countries. In these, the flag is twice as wide as it is tall.

1:1

2:3

1:2

CONSTRUCTION SHEETS

Flag designs are shown on a kind of drawing called a construction sheet. This shows the exact size, shape and position of every part of the design. Some flag designs, such as Poland, are very simple. Others, such as Eswatini, have much more complex designs.

Eswatini

Qatar

Qatar wins the award for narrowest national flag.

EUROPE

The blue band on Liechtenstein's flag represents the sky. The red is for the evening fires that warm this tiny Alpine nation, while a golden crown represents the unity of the people and the prince.

When you think of the history of Europe, perhaps the vast Roman Empire or the adventurous Vikings come to mind. Or maybe you think of the seafaring nations, who sailed across oceans on fleets of ships, waging violent battles. Most European flags are simple – bicolour and tricolour flags make up over half of the continent's national flags. This is because the flags are taken from the days of battles on horseback and at sea, when it was essential to identify, from a distance, who was friend or foe.

Because Europe has a mostly Christian heritage, crosses are shown on many of the nations' flags, particularly in the Scandinavian countries of the north. However, in the far east of the continent, where some countries span Europe and Asia, you'll find flags that share features with Asian flags. Here, the moon and star of Islam shines out from the flags of Türkiye and Azerbaijan.

The Belarusian flag features an intricate pattern based on the traditional rushnik, a ceremonial cloth. Most Belarusian babies receive a rushnik at birth, as the red represents life.

Historians believe that the Russian tricolour is based on the Dutch flag. One theory is that Peter the Great (Tsar of Russia 1682–1725) was so impressed by the fluttering flag on a Dutch boat, he decided to make it his own.

THREE FLAGS IN ONE

The United Kingdom is sometimes called a country of countries as it has four parts: England, Scotland, Wales and Northern Ireland. The national flag, known as the Union Jack or Union Flag, is made up of the red cross of England's Saint George, the diagonal red cross of Ireland's Saint Patrick, and the blue and white cross of Scotland's Saint Andrew.

A UNION OF CROWNS

England and Scotland had been separate kingdoms – often at war with each other and redrawing their borders – for centuries. A union seemed unlikely. However, in 1503, James IV of Scotland married Margaret, the eldest daughter of Henry VII of England. Exactly a century later, the English throne had a lack of immediate heirs. Due to the earlier royal marriage, King James VI of Scotland became King James I of England, unifying the crowns.

FIRST UNION FLAGS

Despite the 'union of crowns', the two kingdoms were still technically separate states. King James however wanted a common symbol. The sensible choice was to combine the English and Scottish flags, but the nations squabbled about which flag should be on top. Eventually they went with the English version.

St Andrew's Cross (Scotland) | St George's Cross (England)

Version preferred in Scotland | Version preferred in England

This early version was sometimes called the Union Flag or King's colours.

THE ADDITION OF IRELAND

After Oliver Cromwell became Lord Protector of the Commonwealth of England, Scotland and Ireland in 1653, an Irish harp was sometimes added to the flag.

In 1801, the red cross of St Patrick was added to the flag when the United Kingdom of Great Britain and Ireland was officially formed after an Act of Union.

Wales

St Patrick's Cross

FLAGS OF THE BRITISH ISLES

The red dragon symbolises the fearlessness of the Welsh people. It has been an **emblem** of Wales since the reign of Cadwaladr, King of Gwynedd, from 655 CE. At the time of the union of crowns, Wales was considered part of England, and was represented by the Cross of St George.

Since 1932, the Isle of Man has been represented by this triskelion – a three-legged symbol. Many say that it is because the island always lands on its feet!

The white stripe in the centre of the Irish flag symbolises peace between the Catholics (green) and Protestants (orange), the two main Christian groups in the country.

This is the final design of the Union Flag!

FROM HEAVENS ABOVE

Legend goes that in 1219, the invading Danes were losing in a battle near Lindanise (now Tallinn, Estonia). Suddenly, a lambskin banner with a white cross fell from the sky. With the cross signalling that God was on their side, King Valdemar II and his army fought on to a miraculous victory. To this day, the Danes have kept their lucky *Dannebrog* ('Danish flag'), making it the oldest national flag currently in existence.

THE RAVEN BANNER

Before the *Dannebrog*'s miraculous appearance, the Vikings of northern Europe often used a raven banner. Ravens were a sign of battle success, as they would flock to battlefields when the victors rode home. Odin, the Norse god of war, also had two ravens called *Huginn* (Thought) and *Muninn* (Memory) who brought news to their master of battles and events across the region.

NORDIC CROSSES

Over time, the cross on the Danish flag shifted from the centre of the flag towards the hoist, and neighbouring countries began using similar designs when they gained **independence**. This specific cross became known as the Nordic cross.

Sweden

A GOLDEN CROSS

The Swedish flag supposedly arose when King Eric IX saw a golden cross in the sky as he landed in Finland for battle in 1157. The cross against the blue sky was also seen as a sign from God for battle success. Whether this is fact or fiction, Sweden's use of yellow and blue can be traced back to Magnus III's coat of arms in 1275.

Denmark

NORDIC NEIGHBOURS

From the 16th to the early 19th century, Norway was in union with Denmark, so the *Dannebrog* flew over Norway. But in 1821, Norway decided it needed a flag of its own. The designer Frederick Meltzer's colour selection was inspired by the US, UK and Netherlands' flags, as those were countries he believed represented freedom.

Norway

LAND OF LAKES

Before Finland achieved independence, a Finnish yacht club flew a white flag with a blue cross. Artists Eero Snellman and Bruno Tuukkanen are credited with the final flag design, which has been flying since 1918. A Finnish poet says that the flag represents the blue of Finland's lakes – fitting for a country with almost 200,000 of them!

Finland

FIRE AND ICE

When Iceland became independent from Denmark in 1944, they too adopted a flag based on the *Dannebrog*. Red represents the fire from Iceland's volcanoes, white is for the ice and snow that often covers the country, and blue represents the surrounding Atlantic Ocean.

Faroe Islands

FLAG OF FREEDOM

Denmark's Faroe Islands have their own language and flag. White represents the foam of the sea and the brightness of the sky, while red and blue show their brotherhood with Nordic nations. During World War II when Denmark was occupied by Germany, the Faroese people flew their own flag to demonstrate they were free.

Iceland

A FLAG FOR A FLEET

With its famous seafaring history, it makes sense that Spain's flag, known as *la Rojigualda*, began life in 1785 with the Spanish navy. It was chosen by King Charles III who picked it out of 12 designs by a naval officer called Antonio Valdés y Bazán. The flag was eventually made the official national flag by Queen Isabella II in 1843.

COAT OF ARMS

The current coat of arms has been used since 1981. The central shield represents the old kingdoms that united to form Spain, while the crown on top symbolises today's **monarchy**. On either side stand the Pillars of Hercules and the Spanish motto, *Plus Ultra* (meaning 'more beyond', another nod to Spain's history of exploration).

A SHORT-LIVED FLAG

From 1931 to 1939 the Spanish monarchy was abolished and the country became a **republic**. For eight years, a new flag flew: this one also featured a coat of arms but on a red, yellow and purple tricolour, representing all parts of Spain. It wasn't to last. Today Spain has a king once more and the red and yellow flag flies again.

They SHALL NOT pass!

THE LEGACY OF AN EMPIRE

The Spanish navy helped create the vast **Spanish Empire**, which included large parts of North and South America as well as areas of Africa, Asia and Oceania. Although this brought ships full of gold and silver to Spain, it was devastating for **indigenous** people in captured lands. Today, independence from Spain is celebrated in the colours and symbols of many South American flags.

BOLD AND PROUD

Several old kingdoms joined together to form Spain. The people of each region still celebrate their unique identities and have great pride in their regional flags. The Catalan flag, known as the *Senyera*, is based on the coat of arms of the Crown of Aragon. The Basque flag, the *Ikurriña*, has a red field that represents its people, a green cross to symbolise freedom and a white cross for God.

Basque Country

Catalonia

A NATION OF NAVIGATORS

Portugal stretches along the Atlantic coast and, like Spain, also has strong links to the sea. In the 15th century, Portugal expanded its fleet in its mission to take over the seas. Its flag features an armillary sphere – a tool that allowed Portuguese sailors to navigate their way around the world's oceans by working out the position of the Sun and stars at different times of year.

THE FAMOUS TRICOLORE

Liberté, egalité, fraternité! France's famous red, white and blue flag, the *Tricolore*, is forever linked with the values of freedom, equality and brotherhood. Its origins begin in the French Revolution of 1789, when the peasants and middle class wanted the same rights as higher classes and rose up to overthrow the monarchy.

PARISIAN COLOURS

Early on in the revolution, a group of Parisians took control of the Bastille, a prison fortress. Among this group were the Paris militia who wore red and blue cockades on their hats. These traditional colours of Paris soon symbolised the revolution. White, representing purity, was added later. By 1794, the official flag design we know today was born.

What's a cockade, anyway?

This is! It's a colourful decoration which shows that the wearer belongs to a particular group.

ALL THAT FOR A NAPKIN!
Following the Franco-Prussian war of 1870, a man called Henri Comte de Chambord was asked by the new parliament to become king. He said he would only do so if France changed its flag back to a white one, representing the monarchy. The French loved their *Tricolore* so they refused. The Catholic Pope apparently commented, "And all that for a napkin!"

WHICH BLUE?
In 1976, the French president decided to use a version of the *Tricolore* with a lighter blue. Since then, both the old and new versions have been used, but it's still more common to see the darker colours fluttering in the breeze.

COPYCAT TRICOLOURS
The French flag might be the most famous tricolour, but it isn't the oldest. French revolutionaries apparently took inspiration from the Dutch flag, which was made of horizontal stripes of red, white and blue. The flag of Luxembourg, which used to be part of the Netherlands, is also very similar. The tricolour design has proved very popular in Europe, with the continent flying a total of seven vertical and 14 horizontal tricolour flags!

Netherlands

Luxembourg

Belgium

Germany

CONTRASTING NEIGHBOURS
Two of France's neighbours have similar flags to the *Tricolore*, but with different colours. Belgium's black, yellow and red vertical stripes date from 1831 and come from a historic coat of arms featuring a golden lion with red claws. Meanwhile, Germany's flag of horizontal black, red and gold was first flown during the 1848 revolution. It became the national flag in 1919 and again in 1949, after World War II.

UNITING A NATION

Though Italy is steeped in history, from the ancient Romans to the great artists and thinkers of the Renaissance and beyond, you'll be surprised to learn that it's actually a fairly new country. Its different regions were only unified in 1870, just over 150 years ago. Since then, Italy's classic flag has grown to be recognised across the globe, bringing to mind historical cities, beautiful landscapes and, of course, delicious pizza. So where did the famous flag's journey begin?

THANKS, NEIGHBOUR!

When Napoleon Bonaparte invaded Italy in 1796, he brought with him the French *Tricolore*, which is thought to have inspired the Italian national flag. The first version – with horizontal stripes – appeared in 1797. Since then, there have been several versions, but all used the green, red and white we know today. The current flag was adopted in 1946, when Italy got rid of its monarchy and became a republic.

WHY GREEN?

The only difference between the Italian flag and the French is that the left stripe is green, not blue. But why? Historians think that it comes from the green and white uniforms worn by the militia in Milan, the capital city of the area invaded by Napoleon.

Who's Napoleon? Me, of course! I'm a French military leader with big ambitions. In a few years, I'll become Emperor of the French and King of Italy.

GREEN, RED AND WHITE

Today, different people give different meanings to the Italian flag colours. Some say green is for freedom, white for faith, and red for love. Others think green represents the Italian countryside, white for the snowy Alps, and red for the blood of the people. Which meaning would you choose?

A COUNTRY WITHIN A COUNTRY

If you travel to the Vatican in the Italian city of Rome, you'll spot a different country's flag. At just under half a square kilometre, Vatican City has been the world's smallest independent country since 1929. It is ruled by the Pope, who is the head of the Catholic Church. Its square flag features the keys of heaven and a crown worn by popes in the past.

SAN MARINO

You might think one tiny country-inside-a-country was enough, but Italy has two! In the mountains of northeast Italy, near the coast, is San Marino, the fifth smallest country in the world. Measuring a little over 61 square kilometres, San Marino was founded by Saint Marinus in 301 CE when he built a monastery in the area. Its bicolour flag features the country's coat of arms, showing the three towers that surround the capital city, also called San Marino, and topped with a crown to represent the country's independence.

WHAT DO FLAG COLOURS MEAN?

Whether a flag's colours have come from a country's history, or have been chosen to represent the hopes of a newly independent nation, they are always full of symbolism.

THE COLOURS OF NATURE

Blue sea, green forests and yellow sun – colours are often used to represent a country's landscape and climate. Argentina's flag commemorates an uprising that led to the country's independence. On the day of the uprising, the clouds over Buenos Aires parted, revealing a blue sky.

Argentina

MATCHING COLOURS

Countries with a history and culture in common often share flag colours too. For example in the colours of **Pan-Arab** flags (page 26) and **Pan-African** flags (page 54).

RED

In many flags, red stands for power, courage, bloodshed and struggle for independence, but it can also stand for equality and brotherhood. The colour is also a famous symbol of **communism** and **socialism**, such as in the flags of China and Vietnam.

Niger · Côte d'Ivoire

ORANGE

Orange is a flag colour you don't see very often! On the flag of Sri Lanka, it represents the Hindu Tamil community. In the flags of Niger and Côte d'Ivoire, bands of orange symbolise the countries' savannahs.

Myanmar

Colombia

YELLOW

As well as representing the Sun, yellow often stands for gold and wealth or natural resources, such as crops. Yellow in the flag of Myanmar stands for solidarity, while in Colombia's flag it stands for liberty and justice.

BLUE

While blue often represents the sea or sky, it can also stand for wealth, as seen in the flag of Laos; for brotherhood, as in the flag for Honduras; or for monarchy, as in the flag of Thailand.

PURPLE

Purple is the rarest colour, found on only four national flags. Discover why on page 50!

GREEN

Green is the colour of nature, so it often represents forests and farmland, for example on the flags of Grenada, Sierra Leone and the Solomon Islands. As the colour brings to mind spring and new life, it is sometimes used to symbolise hope, faithfulness and wisdom, such as on the flags of Belarus and Hungary. It is also an important colour in Islam (see page 38).

WHITE

White often symbolises peace, purity and unity. South Korea's flag features a white background for peace, Indonesia's bicolour flag has white for purity and red for courage, and Singapore's flag symbolises equality.

Learn the story behind Ghana's black star symbol on page 60!

BLACK

In the symbolism of pan-Arab colours, black is said to represent the defeat of enemies. In other flags, such as that of Estonia, it can stand for past suffering or hardships.

ASIA

Sri Lanka's flag features a lion, supposedly because the nation's first ruler brought a lion banner from India in 486 BCE.

Lebanon's flag features its national symbol, the cedar tree. Cedars represent strength and wealth and are mentioned in the Bible.

Asia covers almost a third of our planet's land area and is home to an amazing variety of landscapes and cultures, from the elevated Tibetan mountains to the metropolis of Singapore. Asia's national flags vary as much as its people and include plenty of religious symbolism. Perhaps this is to be expected from a continent that gave birth to 11 major religions including Islam, Christianity, Buddhism, Hinduism and Sikhism.

Many flags in the Arabian Peninsula (Southwest Asia) contain black, white, green and red. These are the Pan-Arab colours. Individually, each colour represents an Arabian dynasty. Fourteenth-century Iraqi poet Safi al-Din al-Hilli wrote: "White are our acts, black our battles, green our fields, and red our swords."

Turkmenistan's flag is considered the most complex in the world. It features five detailed guls (traditional carpet designs) that represent the five main tribes of the country.

Kyrgyzstan's flag features a blazing sun. The 40 rays represent the 40 tribes who united under national hero Manas to fight the invading Mongolians.

Brunei's flag includes a stylised image of the sultan's royal parasol and is the only national flag to feature an umbrella!

The taegeuk on South Korea's flag represents balance between positive and negative forces.

Cambodia's flag features the incredible temple Angkor Wat. Built in the 1100s, it's one of over a thousand buildings, making it the largest religious structure in the world.

LAND OF THE RISING SUN

Japan has flown flags featuring suns for over a thousand years. This is due, in part, to the country's unique geography. With the vast Pacific Ocean to its east, Japan has spectacular sunrises and the country's name – *Nippon* in Japanese – means 'the sun's origin'.

The Sun also plays an important role in Japan's history, as the emperor is said to be descended from Amaterasu, the sun goddess. It is said that Amaterasu hid in a rock cave before emerging with her radiant light. She is also one of the most important gods in the Shinto religion, which originated in Japan.

NEW YEAR, NEW ERA, NEW FLAG

In the year 701, Emperor Monmu is said to have flown a flag with a golden sun to celebrate the new year, which is perhaps the earliest record of its use. Various designs have been fluttering ever since over land and sea, including the spectacular sight of banners strung on fleets of Japanese warships.

IT'S OFFICIAL, I GUESS?

In 1854, Japan began to open up to the rest of the world and the *Hinomaru* – the flag we know today – was ordered to fly on trade ships to distinguish them from other countries. Japan continued to use the flag, even displaying it in government buildings, but it was still an unofficial national emblem. Over 100 years later in 1999, it became Japan's official flag.

Hinomaru is a nickname for the flag, meaning 'ball of the sun'. The flag is officially called the Nisshōki, 'flag of the sun'. All very sunny!

OFF CENTRE

Until 1999, the sun was not quite in the middle, sitting 1/100th of the way to the hoist. After great debate, it was decided that the sun should be central!

For good luck during exams, schoolchildren wear white hachimaki – headbands featuring the red sun!

FLYING FISH FLAGS

In spring, *koinobori* or 'carp streamers' can be seen fluttering all over Japan to celebrate Children's Day on 5 May. Typically, a black fish represents the father, a red fish the mother, and smaller coloured fish fly for the children. Carps' ability to swim up rivers symbolises determination, courage, and the hope that children will grow up healthily.

RED AND GREEN SUN

Since 1972, another nation has flown a rising sun flag: Bangladesh. The original version featured a golden silhouette of the country, but today the flag has a green background to represent the nation's lush scenery, and a red sun symbolising the new dawn of the nation. Like many flags, its existence emerged during a revolution. After a declaration of independence from Pakistan in March 1971, students and activists rushed to design a flag to claim freedom for their land. It is said that shopkeepers refused to take money for the fabric to make the first flags with the golden map.

A FIVE-STAR FLAG

On 1 October 1949, a flag was hoisted at Tiananmen Square in Beijing by the People's Liberation Army. Mao Zedong, leader of the Communist Party, proclaimed the new People's Republic of China, and a decades-long civil war was finally over. This was the Chinese flag.

A STARRY-EYED DESIGNER

On 4 July 1949, citizens were invited to submit designs for the new republic's flag. Zeng Liansong sat in his attic drafting various versions and was attracted by the stars in the night sky. He thought that the ancient Chinese proverb 'longing for the stars, longing for the moon' captured the spirit of the new republic, and he saw the Chinese Communist Party as a bright guiding star for the nation. The four smaller stars on the Chinese flag represent the people being shown the way by the party's light.

REVOLUTIONARY RED

The flag's striking red background symbolises revolution – an important principle in Mao's philosophy on how China should be governed, and the actual revolution which led to the Chinese Communist Party rising to power. The colour red is often tied to communism but it is also a colour deep-rooted in Chinese culture and associated with luck, happiness and prosperity.

ANCIENT TRADITIONS

Before the People's Republic of China was established, a variety of flags in different shapes and designs flew over the land, much like elsewhere across the Asian continent. One striking design came from the Qing Dynasty (1644–1912): the dragon on the yellow background represents the Chinese Empire.

STAR-STUDDED NEIGHBOURS

Three of China's East Asian neighbours also feature prominent stars in their designs. The five points on Vietnam's star represent farmers, workers, intellectuals, youth and soldiers.

Vietnam

One interpretation of the red star on North Korea's flag is that it symbolises communism. Like China, this **ideology** of how a country should be run is fundamental to the nation's ruling party.

Hong Kong

TWO SYSTEMS, ONE COUNTRY

China bans regional flags with two exceptions: Hong Kong and Macau. Both flags contain the five stars from the Chinese national flag, symbolising their unity as well as their unique regional characteristics.

The flag of Hong Kong has a white five-petalled flower in the centre. The tree this flower blooms on is called *Bauhinia x blakeana* or the Hong Kong orchid tree and, since its discovery in 1880, it has become a national symbol.

A different flower – the lotus – sits centrally on Macau's flag. This aquatic plant is fitting given Macau's long history as an important port, which is represented by the waves below. In the middle, spanning the water, is an image of Macau's famous Governador Nobre de Carvalho Bridge.

North Korea

Myanmar's large white star represents purity, honesty and compassion. Yellow stands for unity and happiness, green for peace and the natural environment, and red for courage and determination. When this flag was raised in 2010, instructions were given to burn the country's former flag!

Macau

Myanmar

GANDHI'S FLAG

More people live in India than in any other country on Earth. This diverse nation, speaking hundreds of languages, is united under a single flag. The *Tiranga*, meaning tricolour, was adopted on 22 July 1947, just weeks before India gained independence from the British Empire.

MULTI-FAITH FLAG

Mahatma Gandhi was a leader and activist who fought for India's independence. He wanted India's flag to be a unifying emblem for all Indians. In 1921, he designed a flag featuring red for India's Hindus and green for its Muslims. A white band was added for all the other faiths and cultures of India.

> A flag represents an ideal... It will be necessary for us Hindus, Muslims, Christians, Jews, Parsis and all others to whom India is their home, to recognise a common flag to live and die for.

SYMBOLIC SAFFRON

In 1931, the colour red was changed to saffron, another important colour in Hinduism. When India finally achieved independence, its flag colours were given new symbolism: saffron for courage and sacrifice, white for peace and truth, and green for faith and chivalry.

WHEELS OF CHANGE

Gandhi encouraged India to become self-reliant by spinning its own cloth out of Indian cotton. A spinning wheel was therefore the perfect emblem for the new flag. By 1947, the spinning wheel had been swapped for a dharma chakra, a Buddhist and Hindu symbol representing progress and the eternal order of the universe.

Dharma chakra

Only one type of cloth is used to make the flag: a hand-spun Indian cloth called khadi.

SOYOMBO SYMBOLISM

The Mongolian flag also features a Buddhist symbol. The *Soyombo* is made up of many parts, each representing different things. The sun and moon, for example, symbolise that Mongolia will exist for eternity, and the yin and yang stand for balance between opposites.

Mongolia

Pakistan

PARTING WAYS

Following its independence from the **British Empire** in 1947, the British government split the region into two countries: India, which was mainly Hindu, and Pakistan, which was mainly Muslim. Pakistan's flag is mostly green with a star and crescent moon. Its white band represents the nation's non-Muslim minorities.

India

SCRIPT AND SWORD

With its bold green background and prominent Arabic inscription, underlined with a thin white sword, the flag of Saudi Arabia stands out from the crowd. The text is the Islamic profession of faith, or *shahadah*: "There is no god but Allah; Muhammed is the Messenger of Allah."

The current flag was designed by Hafiz Wahba and has been used since 1973, but earlier versions date back to the 1700s, often showing the script in a larger size, sometimes with a curved sword below and other times with no sword at all.

FLY TO THE LEFT
Arabic scripts are read from right to left, so the design of the Saudi flag is carefully crafted to ensure the text is always legible in its proper direction, no matter how the flag is displayed.

THE SWORD OF A KING
The sword on the Saudi flag is said to represent the sword of King Ibn Saud, who conquered much of central Arabia and founded Saudi Arabia in 1932, uniting the kingdom of Hejaz and Najd, and parts of eastern and southern Arabia. The weapon is also said to symbolise strictness in applying justice, making it an appropriate emblem for a country ruled by strict laws.

A HOLY FLAG
In many countries, lowering a flag to half-mast is a sign of mourning, but because the *shahada* written on the Saudi flag is holy scripture, lowering it is considered blasphemous (disrespectful to God) and not allowed. It is also forbidden to display the flag on other items, such as mugs or t-shirts, which is seen as disrespectful to Islam.

Not only was King Ibn Saud the founder of Saudi Arabia, he is also the father of every Saudi king there has been since his rule!

RECORD-BREAKING
Saudi Arabia boasts the tallest flagpole in the world, standing at 170 metres, in King Abdullah Square in the city of Jeddah. It flies a flag which is a whopping 33 metres by 49 metres in size!

A decorative Islamic script also features in the flag of Iraq, which proclaims 'God is great'.

FEELING A LITTLE GREEN?

You might think Saudi Arabia's flag has a lot of green on it, but it can't compete with the old flag of Libya. From 1977 to 2011, the Libyan flag was completely green! Today, Libya has a horizontal tricolour with a crescent and star.

Libya

PAN-ARAB NEIGHBOURS

Saudi Arabia is surrounded by many smaller countries that share a lot of history, culture and religious beliefs. You can see the connections in their flags, which display the Pan-Arab colours of green, red, black and white.

Jordan

Kuwait

Oman

35

DOING THINGS DIFFERENTLY

In South Asia, triangles and pennants were once the norm, but when European influence spread across the world, most countries adopted rectangular flags. Nepal is the only country in the world whose flag is not rectangular or square.

UNPACKING THE PENNANT

The shape of Nepal's flag – a **pennant** – is believed to represent the country's mountains. The sun and the moon individually represent rulers of Nepal, and together, the wish for Nepal to last for as long as these celestial objects. The blue outline is a symbol of peace, and crimson red represents the rhododendron, Nepal's national flower.

Many countries have their national emblem on their flag, but Nepal has their flag on their national emblem!

PRAYER FLAGS

Prayer flags can be found hanging at temples and monasteries, in homes and at mountain passes across the Himalayan region. Prayers are printed on the flags, and it is believed that the wind will scatter the good wishes.

LAND OF THE THUNDER DRAGON

Just a yak's trek away from Nepal is the country of Bhutan. It is known in the local language as *Druk Yul* – Land of the Thunder Dragon. And this *druk* is an impressive beast! It's not a fearsome creature like dragons from the West. Instead, it's a guardian spirit.

Bhutan

Yellow represents the king, who wears a yellow silk garment called a *kabney*.

The *druk* is white, which represents the purity of the Bhutanese people.

Orange symbolises Buddhism, the national religion.

A DIFFERENT PALETTE

Bhutan's flag is the only one in the world which doesn't feature red, blue or green. Instead, yellow, white and orange are used.

The pearls in the dragon's claws represent prosperity and wealth!

A GRANDMOTHER'S FLAG

Bhutan's flag was designed by Mayeum Choying Wangmo Dorji, the grandmother of the former queen Ashi Kesang Choden. On her original design, the dragon faced towards the hoist. But later, the direction of the dragon was flipped so that its face was clear to see when the flag was flying.

A DIFFERENT DRAGON

Malta's flag also features a dragon, but you'll need to look very closely to spot it! In the centre of the cross is an image of St George on horseback defeating a dragon.

Malta

FLAGS OF FAITH

In some countries, faith plays a big role in people's daily lives. For others, religion is part of their shared history. So, it's no surprise to discover one-third of national flags contain a religious symbol. Of those, nearly half are Christian and around a third are Muslim. A few are Buddhist or Hindu, only one is Jewish, and some even look to religions of the past.

A CROSS FOR A CRUSADE

Cross symbols developed into flags during the time of the Crusades, beginning in 1095 CE, when European Christian armies waged war against Muslim forces in the Middle East in an effort to capture Jerusalem and the surrounding Holy Land. The crusading armies wore a cross of a different colour to identify the nation they belonged to. This symbol was bold and simple so it could be seen from a distance in the heat of battle.

WHICH CROSS?

Look out for the four main types of cross found on flags around the world:

Nordic cross – found on the flags of Norway, Finland, Sweden, Denmark and Iceland.

Greek cross – found on the flags of Greece, Switzerland and Tonga.

Saltire – found on the flags of Scotland and Jamaica.

Symmetric cross – found on the flags of England, Dominica and Georgia.

CRESCENT MOONS

The Islamic faith is often represented by the crescent moon and star, and you'll find it on the flags of many Muslim countries. The symbol dates back a few hundred years before Islam, but it later became associated with the religion and was featured on the flag of the Ottoman Empire. Beginning in the 14th century, for hundreds of years, this Muslim-led empire ruled what is now Türkiye and a large area surrounding the Mediterranean Sea, and sparked the use of this celestial symbol on other Muslim flags.

FIELDS OF GREEN

Green is an important colour in Islam, where it symbolises paradise, and is said to be the favourite colour of the prophet Mohammed. Look out for it on the flags of Iran, Algeria, Pakistan, Bangladesh, Turkmenistan, Saudi Arabia and Mauritania.

There are 16 national flags that feature the crescent moon, some with stars and some without.

THE STAR OF DAVID

The only flag carrying a Jewish symbol is the flag of Israel, also known as the Zionist flag, which features the six-pointed Star of David. Since Roman times, the star had been a mystical symbol thought to protect against evil spirits and it became important to Judaism in the 17th century. In the late 19th century, Jewish people wanted a flag to represent them, and the Star of David was paired with the blue and white stripes of the Jewish prayer shawl. When the state of Israel was founded in 1948, the Zionist flag was chosen as the national flag.

THE AMERICAS

The Americas are home to a real range of flags, from the maple leaf of Canada in the north to the 'Sun of May' of Argentina in the south. Much of the recent history of these two continents has been shaped by Spain, Britain and France, who fought over what they thought of as the 'New World'. Though these European countries brought their own colours and patterns, indigenous symbolism can still be found in flags across the lands. Many countries gained independence from European empires after hundreds of years, and so their flags are a proud symbol of freedom and ambition for the future.

The lone star set in the canton of Chile's flag is said to be a guide on the path to progress and honour. It also links to the first flag flown in Chile: the war flag of the indigenous Mapuche people.

St Vincent has the only national flag with a letter depicted. Three diamonds are arranged in a 'V' for 'Vincent' and show off the islands' status as 'the gems of the Antilles'.

In Jamaica's flag, black represents the strength and creativity of the people, green the lush vegetation and hope, and gold represents sunshine and the wealth of the nation.

Panama's flag is seen on more ships than any other! Businesses from all around the world register their ships there. Today, more than 8,000 vessels fly the same flag.

THE STAR-SPANGLED BANNER

The Stars and Stripes of the United States of America is perhaps the most instantly recognisable flag the world over. As well as being displayed proudly across the states, it flies at the geographic South Pole and has also been planted on the Moon a whopping six times!

I'm seeing stripes!

On 14 June 1777, the first flag was adopted – nearly a year after the United States' 13 colonies declared independence from Britain. The 13 stripes represent these original colonies, while each star represents a state. The plan had been to add a stripe for each new state, but the flag started to look very stripey! The current flag has flown since 4 July 1960, when the 50th star was added for the state of Hawaii.

MANY DESIGNERS AND NO RULES

For such an iconic symbol, it's funny that no one is sure who designed the American flag! One legend says it was sewn by a lady called Betsy Ross. Another claims it was founding father Francis Hopkinson who demanded payment from the government for his design (they didn't pay up). Most historians agree that many people contributed to the design, which evolved over time. In fact, early flag makers arranged the stars however they liked, so all across the new country, there were many different flags.

STATE FLAGS

Each of the USA's 50 states has its own flag, too!

New Mexico's features a red sun symbol of the indigenous Zia people.

South Carolina's palm tree and moon design can be traced back to 1775, the year before the Declaration of Independence.

California's flag is called the Bear Flag. The bear and the words 'California Republic' date back to when the state broke away from Mexico.

Ohio has the only non-rectangular state flag. The shape is known as a burgee.

CONFEDERATE FLAG

During the American Civil War (1861–65), the Confederate States of the south fought against the Unionists of the north under a different flag. Today the Confederate flag represents pride in the identity of the southern states, but for others it is a symbol of racism and oppression – a reminder that these states were against the abolition of slavery.

EAGLE AND SNAKE

Across America's southern border lies Mexico, whose flag features its national coat of arms in the centre. According to Aztec legend, an eagle perched on a cactus eating a snake was a sign to build Tenochtitlán, the capital city of the Aztec Empire. Today, it's known as Mexico City.

Mexico's flag has always had green, white and red stripes, but the eagle emblem has gone through several changes and at times wasn't included at all! When Mexico hosted the 1968 Olympic Games, they didn't want anyone to confuse its flag with Italy's. Since then, the current eagle and snake emblem has taken pride of place on every Mexican flag.

ORDER AND PROGRESS

When Napoleon invaded Portugal in 1807, the prince regent, Dom João, moved to Brazil, one of Portugal's colonies. Once there, he declared that Brazil was no longer a colony, but a kingdom equal with Portugal. Later on, when Dom João returned home, he left his son, Dom Pedro, in charge of Brazil.

The government in Portugal wanted Brazil to go back to being a colony but Dom Pedro was having none of it! He and many of the Brazilian people didn't want to be controlled by a far-off power and so, on 7 September 1822, Dom Pedro declared Brazil's independence from Portugal and became emperor of the new nation. It was time for the country to have its own flag: a green field with a yellow diamond, featuring the imperial coat of arms.

GREEN AND YELLOW

These days, green is said to represent the lush rainforests, and yellow the gold and other rich minerals found across the land, but that's not why they were originally chosen. Green was the traditional colour of Dom Pedro's family, the House of Braganza, while yellow was one of the colours of his wife's family, the Habsburgs.

House of Braganza

House of Habsburg

A FLAG FIT FOR A REPUBLIC

Brazil had been a monarchy under Dom Pedro but in 1889, it became a republic with an elected government. A new flag was raised and while the colours remained the same, the coat of arms was replaced with a blue globe bearing the motto *Ordem e Progresso*, meaning 'Order and Progress', along with a white star representing each state.

STANDING OUT FROM THE CROWD

Brazil's flag is recognised all around the world. Its vibrant colours are worn by the formidable Brazilian football team and can even be found on its famous Havaianas flip-flops!

THE GOLDEN ARROWHEAD

A little north of Brazil is a much smaller country with a much newer flag, also featuring a lot of green and yellow. In the run-up to Guyana's independence from Britain in 1966, a call went out to design a national flag. Up stepped American student Whitney Smith, who would go on to become a famous **vexillologist**. With a few changes, Smith's design was the winning entry, and it has flown ever since. Though the Guyanese government was slightly surprised to discover that their flag designer wasn't from Guyana!

The flag has become known as the Golden Arrowhead. The arrowhead shape represents a drive towards a golden future and recalls the original inhabitants of Guyana, who used arrows for hunting. In the words of Whitney Smith himself, "green stands for the jungles and fields, white for the many rivers of Guyana; black is for perseverance, and red for nation building".

THE MAPLE LEAF

For centuries, the indigenous people of Canada enjoyed *sinzibukwud* – the sweet sap of the maple tree. When European settlers arrived in the 1500s and 1600s they soon discovered the secrets of the delicious maple. From the mid-1700s the popular tree started appearing on regional flags. However, European flags soon flew over Canada as the British and French both colonised areas of these northern lands. Even after Canada gained independence in 1931, the Union Jack of the United Kingdom continued to soar over the land, sometimes alongside a Canadian ensign.

COMPETITION TIME

In 1964, a contest was held to design a national flag for Canada that would capture the identity of the nation. About two-thirds of the entries included the maple leaf. A committee gathered to narrow the suggestions down to two flags for a final vote. One was the 'Pearson Pennant' – a three-stemmed maple leaf on a white panel surrounded by two blue panels. These colours symbolised the national motto 'from sea to sea', as Canada stretches from the Atlantic Ocean in the east to the Pacific Ocean in the west.

OUR LAND

Nunavut (the Inuktitut word for 'our land') is the northernmost and newest of the Canadian territories, established in 1999. An iconic symbol was chosen to represent the region: the *inuksuk*, a marker made from stones and boulders piled high to look like a figure. The blue star represents the North Star and the leadership of the elders in the community.

OUR FLAG

Greenland is an autonomous territory within the Kingdom of Denmark that neighbours Canada to the northeast. Until 1985, only the *Dannebrog* (see page 16) was flown as the official flag, but that year, Greenland held a contest to create a new design. Many entries featured Nordic crosses to honour the relationship with similar territories, but the winning design bears no cross at all, and is striking and unique.

Called *Erfalasorput* ('our flag'), it was designed by Greenlander Thue Christiansen. The red stripe represents the ocean and the white stripe the icecap. The red semicircle is the sun, and the white semicircle is the pack ice that surrounds Greenland.

THE WINNER!

The simplicity of historian George Stanley's competition entry – a single maple leaf on a red and white triband – won out. It was inspired by the Canadian Royal Military College flag which was also red and white. The two colours honoured the British and French histories respectively, and the maple leaf was a neutral symbol for Canadian peoples of all races and backgrounds.

ONE NATION TWO FLAGS

THE TRICOLOUR

In August 1825, just 11 days after they gained independence from Spain, a red and green striped flag with a yellow star was adopted by Bolivia. On today's design (in use since 2009), red represents the bravery of soldiers who fought for independence, yellow the nation's resources, and green is for the fertile land.

Most nations have additional flags to the 'main' or national flag, for example, there may be flags specifically for use at sea or other state flags for the president and royal family. Since 2009, however, Bolivia has been the only country to have not one but two very different official flags – the tricolour and the *wiphala*.

COAT OF ARMS

Coats of arms are unique designs which are used as symbols of countries, monarchs, regions and even families. South America is a hot spot for flags featuring coats of arms, with five nations displaying theirs proudly. Have a look at what Bolivia displays on theirs below!

- A hat called a Phrygian hood represents freedom
- A wreath made of laurel leaves and an olive branch
- An Andean condor, the national bird
- Six Bolivian flags – three each side
- Cannons signifying Bolivia's strength of defence
- Ten stars representing the nation's ten regions
- A central image featuring a rising sun, two mountains – the Cerro Rico and the Cerro Menor – a chapel, a llama, some wheat and a palm tree

THE WIPHALA

The marvellous *wiphala* symbol has been used by Andean peoples for over a thousand years. It consists of 49 squares of seven different colours. In 2009, Evo Morales, the first indigenous president in South America, declared the *wiphala* to have national flag status alongside the tricolour. With this, indigenous Bolivians were lifted up as citizens and made to feel included in their homeland.

Each colour of the wiphala *has a special meaning.*

Yellow represents energy.

Orange is for society and culture.

Red is for the earth and the Andean people.

Violet is for Andean ideology and politics.

Blue represents the heavens.

Green is for natural resources.

White represents time.

FOUR WIPHALAS

Four different regions or *suyus* each have different *wiphala* patterns. These regions are now parts of present-day Colombia, Ecuador, Peru, Chile and Argentina as well as Bolivia. The west of Bolivia is in the Collasuyo region, so takes the *wiphala* with white squares running down the central diagonal.

49

THE PURPLE PARROT

The beautiful sisserou parrot is only found on the sunny Caribbean island of Dominica, so it's fitting that this bird perches proudly on the country's flag. Sitting in front of a red disc, it represents the country reaching great heights to achieve its ambitions. Ten green stars surrounding the parrot represent Dominica's ten parishes, and the tricoloured cross represents the Christian holy trinity.

COLOURS FOR A COUNTRY

Each colour on Dominica's flag holds a special meaning. The yellow stands for sunshine and the Carib people, whose ancestors lived on the island before colonisation. The black stands for the volcanic island's fertile soil and the African heritage of many Dominicans. White symbolises hope and the island's many rivers. Finally, the green background represents Dominica's tropical forests.

A FLAG OF INDEPENDENCE

Like many of its Caribbean neighbours, Dominica's flag grew from colonial roots. The island was colonised by the French in 1632, and for the next 200 years it was fought over by the French and British, switching back and forth between the two empires. Finally, in 1978 Dominica gained independence, doing away with its old flag with links to the British Empire and hoisting the unique and vibrant flag we see today.

A SPLASH OF PURPLE

The purple of the sisserou parrot's feathers is unusual – not for birds, but for flags. Barely any other country's flag includes the colour! In the past, purple dye was extremely expensive to make as thousands of sea snails were needed to produce even a small amount. It was only used by monarchs and emperors. Since a less expensive purple dye was discovered in the 1850s, a few modern flags now feature the eye-catching colour. If you look closely, you'll also spot it in the flags of Nicaragua and El Salvador, and in the Bolivian *wiphala*.

WHAT'S IN A NAME?

Dominica's modern name comes from the explorer Christopher Columbus, who spotted it from his ship on Sunday, 3 November 1493. In Latin, *dies Dominica* means 'the Lord's Day', another name for Sunday.

ALWIN BULLY

Dominica's flag was designed by the famous playwright, artist, teacher and national treasure Alwin Bully, who spent much of his life working to promote and preserve Dominica's culture.

RED, GOLD, BLACK AND GREEN

Have you noticed that a handful of Caribbean flags contain red, gold, black and green? These are Pan-African colours (see page 54). Although the Caribbean is a long way from Africa, it has strong ties because of the slave trade. From the 16th to 19th century, European slave traders – mainly from Britain and France – enslaved and transported around five million West Africans to the Caribbean to force them to work on sugar plantations. Most slaves were treated horribly, and many died before they had even made it across the Atlantic Ocean. Today, many Caribbean people proudly trace their ancestry back to Africa, and their flags' colours often share the same symbolism.

THE SUN AND MOON

You might expect that countries' flags – so often planted on land or flown at sea – would focus on symbols closer to Earth. In fact, as you've probably already spotted in this book, many flags are emblazoned with a sun or moon. But what do these recurring symbols mean?

SHINING SUNS

As a source of heat, light and energy, the Sun is vital to our existence. It's not so surprising then that it takes centre stage in different forms on flags across the globe. In South America, Inti was the sun god, worshipped throughout the Incan Empire, and today, many modern countries in that region feature the symbol on their flags. Inti can be seen watching over Potosi mountain on the flag of Bolivia, and on the Ecuadorian flag, Inti sits above a mountain and a steamboat floating on the Guayas River. Further south, the blazing *Sol de Mayo* ('Sun of May') on Uruguay's and Argentina's flags also represents the god Inti, as well as the countries' freedom.

Many accounts say Inti was the son of Viracocha, the great creator, who had the sun on his head, thunderbolts in his hands, and rain streaming down his face as tears.

CARIBBEAN SUNRISE

In the Caribbean, Antigua and Barbuda's flag features a sun rising from the sea. Framed within red triangles that form a 'V' for victory, this eye-catching sun represents the dawn of a new era of hope for a newly independent nation.

BLAZING BRIGHT

Across the Atlantic, the theme of freedom continues in Europe. You can't miss the yellow sun that fills North Macedonia's flag, following its independence from Yugoslavia in 1991. It is said to represent the 'new sun of liberty' as sung in the country's **national anthem**.

A NEW DAWN

Travelling down to southern Africa, a red sun rises in the top band of Malawi's flag. Here, the sun represents a new dawn of hope and progress for the country since it gained independence in 1964.

BY THE LIGHT OF THE MOON

We've already looked at how Islam is often represented by the crescent moon; however, there is one flag where the crescent moon holds a different meaning. In the red and white bicolour of Singapore, the moon symbolises the growth of a young nation alongside five stars representing democracy, justice, equality, peace and progress.

FULL MOON FEVER

Full moons are a more unusual sight on flags, but a yellow full moon features prominently on the flag of Palau (and you can find out the story behind it on page 73). The white disc on *Thong Dwang Deaen* (the white moon flag) of Laos not only symbolises the full moon against the Mekong River, but also the country's bright future and unified people. It also honours Japan in helping Laos gain independence.

AFRICA

On Malawi's flag, a sun with 31 rays signifies that it was the 31st African nation to declare independence in 1964.

Africa's vast and vibrant landscape is home to 54 countries – more than any other continent! It's no surprise, then, that it also flies a huge variety of flags. Across the continent, a five-pointed star is a common motif, often representing unity, liberty or life. In the north, many flags display the Pan-Arab colours, showing the relationship with their Middle East neighbours, while in Central and West Africa, the Pan-African colours of red, green and yellow are used. They take inspiration from the flag of Ethiopia, and together represent an ideal that each country strives to achieve.

Over recent centuries, and especially in the late 1800s, Africa was deeply affected by colonisation from European empires which exploited the land's resources and people, and interfered in relations between tribal areas. But in the 20th century, after years of struggle, almost all of the continent gained independence, and with independence came new emblems for many nations. With a troubled colonial history and so many languages, cultures, alliances and rivalries, unity can be a challenge, but Africa's flag families show that its countries still have close ties.

The borders of The Gambia follow the path of the Gambia River, which also takes centre stage on its flag as a blue stripe across the middle.

FOREVER FREE

Ethiopia is a vast country in East Africa, dominated by mountainous highlands, dry lowlands and a stretch of desert. It's unsurprising, then, that this harsh environment has produced some of the toughest warriors on the planet. For centuries, Ethiopians have defended their homeland with fierce pride, and this is seen most clearly during the height of Europe's colonisation of Africa.

In 1870, only 10 per cent of Africa was under European control but by 1914, it was nearly 90 per cent of the continent. During this brutal period of colonisation, Ethiopia stands out as one of the few that successfully maintained its independence.

A FLAG BORN FROM BATTLE

In 1896, Emperor Menelik II and his lion-hearted warriors defeated the invading Italian army at the Battle of Adwa. One year later, Menelik designed a flag for his victorious empire, consisting of a red band for the bloodshed in defence of the homeland, a yellow band for religious freedom and peace, and a green band representing Ethiopia's land and hope.

The letters in the centre are Emperor Menelik's initials in Ge'ez – an ancient Ethiopian language.

A WORLD WAR VICTORY

In 1936, Benito Mussolini, then Prime Minister of Italy, briefly claimed ownership of Ethiopia. The occupation was brutal but local warriors kept fighting for freedom. By 1941, the whole world was engulfed in World War II. The Ethiopian resistance continued to fight and finally, with the support of the British forces and other allied troops, achieved victory that same year. Restored to the throne, Emperor Haile Selassie raised a flag with a lion in the centre, representing the bravery of the people who kept Ethiopia forever free, and his own descent from King Solomon and the Queen of Sheba.

A BRIGHT FUTURE

In place since 1996, the centrepiece of today's flag is a star with five rays. The star represents Ethiopia's bright future, and the rays represent equality among all Ethiopians regardless of race, religion or gender.

COLOURS FOR A CONTINENT

Because of Ethiopia's history of resisting colonisation, the whole of Africa looked towards the country as a symbol of strength. Today, there are 22 other African national flags which use the green, yellow and red of Ethiopia. These are the Pan-African colours.

THE VALUE OF FREEDOM

In 1958, Guinea was one of the first nations to adopt the Ethiopian colours. When gaining independence and unfurling his country's red, yellow and green tricolour, President Ahmed Sékou Touré declared: "We prefer poverty in freedom than riches in slavery."

A FAMILY OF INDEPENDENT NATIONS

After gaining independence in 1960, Cameroon flew its own green, red and yellow flag. In 1975, the flag was redesigned with a single central star to symbolise national unity while still celebrating President Ahmadou Ahidjo's Pan-African vision.

Cameroonians... The great family of independent nations welcomes us... Long live independent Cameroon.

LAND OF WARRIORS

Dressed in red robes, with spears and shields in hand, and living in lands with lions, wildebeest and giraffes, Maasai warriors are an impressive sight. The Maasai people come largely from northern, central and southern Kenya. They are known for showing calmness and courage, even in danger, and for their expert knowledge of the land and wildlife around them.

To this day, many Maasai live a semi-nomadic lifestyle, herding cattle and goats just as their ancestors did for centuries. Nationally and internationally, the Maasai are celebrated for staying true to their traditions. This celebration is shown most prominently on Kenya's flag, which depicts a Maasai *elongo*, or shield.

A WARRIOR'S SHIELD

The *elongo* is made from cow hide stretched and sewn over a wooden platform. Different sub-groups and families were represented by different designs, and in the past, warriors would often use blood to make their red dye. *Elongo* were used in warfare and cattle raids, and provided spiritual as well as physical protection, as elders and leaders would bless a warrior's shield. It's no wonder then that on Kenya's flag, the *elongo* represents defence of the nation.

RIGHTEOUS COLOURS

The colours of the Kenyan flag are also significant to the Maasai people. Traditionally, they believe in one God called Engai, but this God has two personalities: Engai Narok (the Black God) is kind and Engai Na-nyokie (the Red God) is fierce. These righteous colours of black and red have been used by Maasai people for centuries.

A SWAZI SHIELD

The small southern African country of Eswatini also features a shield on its flag. In the centre of the field is a traditional Nguni shield and spears, representing the readiness of the Swazi people to defend their land, culture and traditions. The striking and contrasting black and white segments of the shield symbolise black and white citizens living together in harmony.

The blue feathers that adorn the shield represent the Swazi royal family – a rarity in a continent where the majority of countries have presidents. As well as having a monarch, Eswatini breaks away from Pan-African colour conventions using sky blue, instead of green, to represent peace and stability. Yellow stands for Eswatini's resources and red for bloodshed in the nation's past battles.

BLACK, RED AND GREEN

Black, red and green are also the colours of the Kenya African National Union (KANU), the party that led Kenya's fight for freedom. Black for the people, red for the struggle and green for the land. The rooster represents the arrival of a new day. Upon independence in 1963, the rooster was replaced with the Maasai *elongo* and white lines were added to symbolise peace for this newly free nation.

A SYMBOL OF FREEDOM

From the late 1950s to 1980, groups of people fought valiantly across the African continent to gain independence for their country. This was called **decolonisation**. In 1957, Ghana was the first sub-Saharan African nation to gain independence and a competition was held so the newly liberated citizens could design their flag.

RED, GOLD AND GREEN

Theodosia Okoh, a talented artist and teacher, won the competition to design a striking Ghanaian flag featuring the Pan-African colours. The red band symbolises the bloodshed in the country's fight for independence, the yellow band represents the nation's gold resources, and the green reflects Ghana's rich forests. These colours pay homage to Ethiopia, a country that fiercely resisted **colonialism** and stood as a symbol for hope and freedom in Africa.

BLACK STAR

In 1919, a Jamaican activist called Marcus Garvey formed a shipping company called the Black Star Line. Owned and run by local people, it became a symbol for freedom and independence. In Ghana, the black star can be seen everywhere – from its prominent place on the flag to landmarks like Black Star Gate in Black Star Square and the national football team: the Black Stars!

NEW FLAGS FOR NEW BEGINNINGS

Because **decolonisation** happened relatively recently, we can pinpoint the origin stories of all these African flags. The talented designers all had a unique opportunity to write their nation's new history.

SOMALIA

Mohammed Awale Liban, a scholar, designed the flag of Somalia following the country's independence in 1954. Its five-pointed star represents the five areas where the Somali people live, and the light blue, originally chosen in honour of the United Nations, today represents the sky and the sea beside the country.

TOGO

Artist Paul Ahyi designed the Togolese flag. The white star represents peace and hope, and marked the country's freedom from colonial rule in 1960.

Ahyi also designed the Independence Monument in Togo's capital, Lomé.

NAMIBIA

Namibia gained its independence in 1990. A flag competition was launched, but rather than picking one winner, the government used the colours and meanings from three designers: Theo Jankowski's message of hope, Don Stevenson's Sun symbol, and Ortrud Clay's design celebrating peace.

A FLAG FOR A FRESH START

With its six bold blocks of colour, South Africa's flag is one of the most striking and colourful in the world. When it was first hoisted on 27 April 1994, it marked a turning point for a deeply divided country. Black South Africans had finally won the right to vote, electing a new government led by President Nelson Mandela and ending the terrible apartheid system.

The old South African flag was a symbol of colonialism as it was based on the flag of the Netherlands, as well as including the British Union Jack. It was time for a new flag to represent all South Africans, especially those who had not been given a voice in their great nation.

JOINING TOGETHER

The new flag was designed by Frederick Brownell, a **state herald**. He explained that the colours and Y-shape represent a joining together of the country's past and present, and all its different people. Black, green and yellow were the colours of the African National Congress – the new ruling political party. Red, white and blue were the colours of the British and Afrikaners from South Africa's colonial past. Red, white, black, green and yellow were colours of the Zulus – one of the largest ethnic groups in South Africa, while green was also a colour of Islam. But in the flag's design, none of the colours represent a specific group. Instead, together, they encompass all South Africans.

WHAT WAS APARTHEID?

Deep racial inequalities existed in South Africa since it was first colonised by the Dutch, but from 1948 until 1994, the government set up a system of laws, known as apartheid, that aimed to keep different races separate. White people, who were a minority, held the wealth and power. Black, mixed race and Indian people were not allowed to live, socialise, or go to school in the same places. Their jobs were restricted, and they were not allowed to vote. Nelson Mandela was one of many activists who fought long and hard to abolish apartheid, even spending 27 years in prison for the cause. By the end of his life, he was considered a hero around the world.

CRAYONS AT THE READY!

When the new flag design was sent by fax machine to Nelson Mandela for approval, it was printed in black and white. Somebody had to quickly buy colouring pencils and colour in the fax!

HATS OFF TO LESOTHO

The small mountainous country of Lesotho is completely surrounded by South Africa. Its flag features a traditional Sotho straw hat, called a *mokorotlo*, as an emblem of the country. It was first flown in 2006 to celebrate the 40th anniversary of the country's independence from Great Britain.

A FLAG MENAGERIE

It seems natural that a creature displayed on a flag should be thought of as majestic and fearless, so it's no surprise to discover that the most common bird featured is an eagle. And if that isn't fierce enough for you, how about one with two heads?

DOUBLE-HEADED EAGLE

Skanderbeg, the national hero of Albania who defeated the Ottomans, was part of the Kastrioti family. Their emblem featured a two-headed eagle and now the double-headed eagle represents the entire nation. Neighbouring Montenegro and nearby Serbia also include a two-headed eagle on their flags.

AN EGYPTIAN EAGLE

In the 12th century, Saladin became the first sultan of Egypt and Syria. The Eagle of Saladin then found its way back onto the Egyptian flag in 1952, following the Egyptian Revolution.

The flags of Zambia, Moldova and Mexico also feature an eagle!

On the flag of Kazakhstan, a steppe eagle soars towards the Sun, symbolising freedom.

BIRDS, BIRDS AND MORE BIRDS

Birds are found on lots of flags. On the flag of Uganda, their national bird – a grey crowned crane – proudly stands to attention. Ecuador's flag features an Andean condor perched on its coat of arms, while on the Guatemalan flag, a native quetzal sits on a scroll.

HOOVES, HORNS AND FUR

You'll find some interesting four-legged beasts hiding in coats of arms – but you'll have to look closely to spot them! On the flag of Venezuela is Palomo, the white horse of Simón Bolívar, who led the country to independence from the Spanish Empire. The state flag of Peru features a vicuña – related to llamas and alpacas, this animal represents freedom and national pride.

Over in Europe, the country of Andorra features two red cows on its flag. Andorra was once governed by France and Spain, and the cows represent those found in the French region of Béarn. Not to be outdone, Croatia has three different species on its flag: three lion heads, a goat and a marten at the top of its coat of arms, representing its historic regions.

THE LION'S ROAR

Seen as courageous and regal, the lion often features on coats of arms. It's on the flag of Jersey in the Channel Islands, Bermuda in the North Atlantic and the Cayman Islands in the Caribbean. These are all British territories, meaning they were once part of the British Empire and still have ties to the United Kingdom. That's why their flags include the lion from the English royal coat of arms.

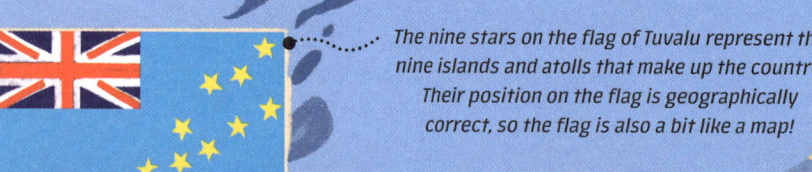

The nine stars on the flag of Tuvalu represent the nine islands and atolls that make up the country. Their position on the flag is geographically correct, so the flag is also a bit like a map!

OCEANIA

As you might guess from its name, Oceania covers a vast area of ocean. However, out of all the continents, it has the smallest land area and the fewest people living there (not counting Antarctica!). Surrounded by so much water, it's no wonder that the countries' flags are connected to the sea. Most flags feature the colour blue and, in most cases, this symbolises the ocean. Stars also feature on several flags, as the seafaring peoples of the region have looked to the skies for navigational guidance for thousands of years. However, not all the stars represent the same thing: some are position markers, while others show the Southern Cross or the Commonwealth Star.

Many countries in Oceania only became independent from the United Kingdom, United States and Australia in the 1970s and 80s. While you can find nods to these countries on some flags today, many designs reflect these nations' own unique local cultures, from full moon fishing parties to a beautiful bird of paradise or the tusk of a wild boar.

The flag of Tonga dates to the 1840s, when King George 'Iron Cable' Tupou I ruled the nation. Since 1875, the constitution has stated that it must never be altered.

The four Federated States of Micronesia are each represented by a star in its flag. Together, they form the four points of a compass.

Kiribati's flag features a local frigatebird soaring across the waves over a blazing sun. The bird symbolises freedom, command of the ocean and special Kiribati dance patterns.

The flag design of Nauru was chosen when the country gained independence in 1968. The yellow line symbolises the Equator, while the white star represents the island's position just 40 kilometres to the south.

The coat of arms on Fiji's flag mixes British and Fijian symbols. The Cross of St George and the lion wearing a crown are British, but the lion is holding a cocoa pod, and there are images of sugar cane, a coconut palm and bananas, which all grow in Fiji.

THE SOUTHERN CROSS

On every clear night across the Southern Hemisphere, a beautiful set of stars can be seen adorning the sky. This constellation has acted as a celestial signpost for centuries, guiding those wandering the outback on foot and those navigating the seas in canoes or sailing boats.

The Māori of Aotearoa call this constellation *Te Pae Mahutoka* and view it as the anchor of a sky canoe. According to an Aboriginal legend, it is part of an emu stretching across the sky. Much later, European settlers called it the Southern Cross. However, it's clear that across the region this brilliant constellation is shared and celebrated, as seen by the flags of Australia and New Zealand.

THE AUSTRALIAN FLAG

In 1901, a competition was held to design the Australian flag, but there were restrictions: designs were strongly advised to feature the Union Flag and the Southern Cross, and they had to have a blue background. Naturally, several people created similar designs and, in the end, five people created flags with so few differences that they were all declared winners!

INDIGENOUS FLAGS

The Aboriginal Flag was designed in 1970 by Harold Thomas, a descendant of the Luritja people from Central Australia. Black symbolises the indigenous peoples of Australia, red stands for earth and the yellow circle represents the Sun. Amid long-awaited progress in recognition of rights for indigenous people, the Aboriginal flag received 'Flag of Australia' status in 1995, as did the flag of the Torres Strait Islanders, another indigenous group.

SIX STARS

The five stars towards the fly on the Australian flag depict the Southern Cross, and towards the hoist sits a Commonwealth Star. This seven-pointed star represents the union of the separate colonies which joined to make Australia. Six points stand for the original states, and the seventh represents Australia's territories.

THE NEW ZEALAND FLAG

In 1830, a ship carrying two Māori chiefs among its passengers was seized by Australian officers for not flying a flag but, at the time, New Zealand didn't have one. In 1834, 25 Māori chiefs and 13 British and American ship captains, missionaries and settlers agreed on the flag of the United Tribes of New Zealand. New Zealand's current flag was adopted in 1902. It notes the historical ties to the UK, but also displays four stars representing the meaningful Southern Cross constellation.

MĀORI FLAG

The Māori are the indigenous people of Aotearoa – the name for New Zealand in te reo – and their flag is often seen alongside New Zealand's national flag, especially at events such as Waitangi Day. The swirling shape represents a curling fern frond, which symbolises the unfolding of new life and hope for the future.

TIME FOR A CHANGE?

People have questioned whether New Zealand's flag and its inclusion of the Union Flag is right for an independent country. In 2016, citizens were asked to select an alternative flag. A blue and black design featuring a silver fern resonated with the people. Black has long been associated with New Zealand, notably the All Blacks rugby team. The silver fern is unique to New Zealand and Māori consider the plant a sign of strength. When it came time to decide between the new and current flag, the original narrowly won out.

A COLOURFUL COUNTRY

Papua New Guinea is a country steeped in uniqueness. Located on the world's second biggest island, it is home to over 1,000 different groups of people who speak more than 800 different languages! Across the country, different tribes gather for events called Sing-Sings, where people share and celebrate their cultures and traditions by singing and dancing. Diversity is not limited to the people either: over 5 per cent of the world's species can be found in the lush Papua New Guinean rainforests, including singing dogs, tree kangaroos, egg-laying mammals and rainbowfish.

THE BIRD OF PARADISE

Possibly the most spectacular of all animals that call this country home is the bird of paradise, Papua New Guinea's national bird. This colourful creature is a beloved symbol for a colourful country, and it has long been used by the regional government and on regional flags. Its long and colourful feathers are used by some tribes in headdresses and clothing, and Papua New Guinea's rugby team is even nicknamed the Kumuls, which means 'bird of paradise' in the language Tok Pisin.

A MECHANICAL MISFIT

Before Papua New Guinea gained independence in 1975, the country operated under the control of Australia for almost 60 years. During this time, a new flag was proposed: a blue, yellow and green tricolour. Blue stood for the surrounding oceans and islands, gold stood for the country's coasts, mineral wealth and unity, and green represented the forests on the mainland. It also featured the Southern Cross, much like Australia's flag. But this proposal was not liked at all. The people decided that the flag looked too 'mechanical' and didn't capture the nation's spirit or essence.

A TALENTED TEEN

In 1971, Susan Karike, a 15-year-old schoolgirl, drew a design for a new national flag featuring a bird of paradise soaring high, showing the nation rising in prosperity. She also added the Southern Cross, demonstrating the strong bond with other South Pacific countries. The colours of red and black are divided diagonally – a rare sight on national flags – and are traditionally used in costumes of the different Papuan peoples. She submitted her design to the country's flag contest and was swiftly declared the winner.

HOPE AND PEACE

Timor-Leste, one of the world's newest nations and a near neighbour of Papua New Guinea, flies a flag featuring the same colours. When the design was adopted in 1975, the meaning of each colour was a fresh reminder: black represented 400 years of colonialism and red represented the people's spilled blood. The yellow arrow marked the struggle for independence and the white star symbolised hope for a better future.

In 2002, when the flag was reinstated after the end of Indonesia's occupation, the colours took on new meaning: yellow celebrated the country's wealth and the white star was a guiding light and represented peace.

THE BOAR'S TUSK FLAG

Far out in the south Pacific Ocean you'll find Vanuatu. This country, formed of a group of volcanic islands, has flown its distinctive flag since it gained independence from the United Kingdom and France in 1980. The most unique part of the flag is the emblem of a boar's tusk encircling the leaves of a *namele* tree – a symbol steeped in the traditions of the local people, who are known as Ni-Vanuatu.

A TREASURED TUSK

The boar's tusk is a local symbol of prosperity. To achieve such spectacular circular teeth, the owner of a boar must remove the pig's upper teeth then care for the growth of the lower teeth over many years, eventually feeding the animal by hand. In Vanuatu culture, the more pigs a man has, the higher his status. When the pig is sacrificed, the meat is shared with all the other villagers at a feast, and the boar's tusks are worn as a pendant.

LEAVES OF PEACE

The *namele* leaves are a token of peace. You'll have to look very closely to count them, but the 39 segments on the flag represent the original 39 members of Vanuatu's parliament.

BOLD COLOURS

The colours of red, green, yellow and black stem from the flag of Vanua'aku Pati, the political party that led Vanuatu to independence. Green represents the lush, fertile lands, while red symbolises the blood of the pigs sacrificed in religious rituals on the islands. Yellow stands for sunshine, peace and the light of Christianity, and black represents both the rich volcanic soil and the country's native Melanesian people.

WHY THE 'Y'?

Notice how the pattern on Vanuatu's flag is similar to South Africa's? In fact, that's just a coincidence. Here, the Y-shape reflects the layout of the islands, as well as symbolising Christianity spreading through the island chain.

FULL MOON FISHING

Vanuatu is by no means the only Pacific country to have a flag steeped in the culture of the local people. Behind Palau's simple yet striking flag is an incredible story. Each month around the time of the full Moon, there is a spectacular sight in the waters surrounding Palau. Tens of thousands of fish called red snappers gather to perform their mating ritual. Not surprisingly, this in turn attracts many predators, such as sharks. All this action makes the full Moon a prime time for fishing, and it is also considered the best time for sowing, harvesting and celebrating. To reflect its importance in Palau culture, the full Moon above the ocean waters has filled the country's flag since 1981.

FUN FLAG ODDITIES

With 195 independent countries across six continents, that's an awful lot of flags! We haven't even scratched the surface of the many more flags flown in different regions. Do you have a favourite? Maybe you've discovered one in this book that takes your fancy, or perhaps the flag of your own country holds a place in your heart. Here are a few more fun and unusual flag facts you might not know about. So, if you ever take a flag quiz, you're bound to pass with flying colours...

Paraguay

Paraguay is one of only three national flags with a different design on the front and back. The national coat of arms is shown on the front, while on the back there is the seal of the **treasury**.

Vatican City and Switzerland are the only countries with square flags.

Vatican City

What's great about living in Switzerland? Well, it's flag is a big plus!

Switzerland

You would be forgiven for mixing up these three flags – they're almost identical!

The Polish flag is the same as the flag of Indonesia, just with the colours flipped upside down. Indonesia and Monaco have the same design, but the shape of Monaco's is a bit narrower.

Poland **Indonesia** **Monaco**

The Jamaican flag is the only national flag in the world not to feature red, white or blue.

The flag of the Philippines is unique as it is turned upside down during times of war. In peace, the flag is flown with the blue band on top. However, during war, the flag is displayed with the red band on top, representing courage and the nation's readiness to defend itself.

Belize is one of only two independent nations to feature people on its flag. The other is Malta, which has a tiny image of St George defeating a dragon (see page 37). You can also find a woman with a cross and a harp on the flag of Montserrat, an island territory in the Caribbean.

The black and white stripes on the flag of Botswana represent the stripes of the country's national animal, the zebra. They also symbolise harmony between people of different ethnicities.

On New Year's Day each year, the US flag in Antarctica is repositioned to keep it on the Geographic South Pole. This is because the ice moves about 10 metres every year.

The world record for biggest flag goes to Romania. In 2013 it rolled out a flag that was a whopping 349 metres long and 227 metres wide – that's bigger than three football pitches.

DESIGN YOUR OWN FLAG

Now you've learned the stories behind many of the world's flags and the meaning of their symbols and colours, why not design your own flag? It could represent your family, where you live, or maybe it could be a flag for Planet Earth... just in case an alien spaceship comes along and needs to know where they are!

FLAG INDEX

EUROPE

- Albania — 64
- Andorra — 12, 65
- Armenia — 26
- Austria — 12
- Azerbaijan — 12, 39
- Belarus — 12, 25
- Belgium — 12, 21
- Bosnia & Herzegovina — 12
- Bulgaria — 12
- Croatia — 12, 65
- Cyprus — 12, 13
- Czech Republic — 12
- Denmark — 12, 17, 38
- Estonia — 14-15, 38
- Finland — 13, 17, 38
- France — 13, 20-21, 40, 51, 65, 72
- Georgia — 13, 38
- Germany — 13, 17, 21
- Greece — 13, 38
- Hungary — 13, 25
- Iceland — 13, 17, 38
- Ireland — 13, 15
- Italy — 13, 22-23, 56
- Latvia — 13
- Liechtenstein — 12
- Lithuania — 12
- Luxembourg — 12, 21
- Malta — 12, 37
- Moldova — 12, 64
- Monaco — 12, 13, 74
- Montenegro — 12, 64
- Netherlands — 12, 17, 21, 62
- North Macedonia — 12, 53
- Norway — 12, 17, 38
- Poland — 11, 12, 74
- Portugal — 12, 19, 44
- Romania — 13, 75
- Russia — 12, 13
- San Marino — 13, 23
- Serbia — 13, 64
- Slovakia — 13
- Slovenia — 13
- Spain — 13, 18-19, 40, 48, 65
- Sweden — 13, 17, 38
- Switzerland — 11, 13, 38, 74
- Türkiye — 13
- Ukraine — 13
- United Kingdom — 13, 14, 15, 46, 65, 66, 72
- Vatican City — 23, 74

ASIA

- Afghanistan — 26
- Bahrain — 26
- Bangladesh — 26, 29
- Bhutan — 26, 37
- Brunei — 26, 27
- Cambodia — 26, 27
- China — 8, 24, 26, 28, 30-31
- India — 8, 26, 32-33
- Indonesia — 25, 26, 74
- Iran — 27, 39
- Iraq — 27, 38
- Israel — 27, 39
- Japan — 27, 28-29, 53
- Jordan — 27, 35
- Kazakhstan — 27, 64
- Kuwait — 27, 35
- Kyrgyzstan — 9, 27
- Laos — 25, 27, 53
- Lebanon — 26, 27
- Malaysia — 27, 39
- Maldives — 26, 39
- Mongolia — 26, 27, 33
- Myanmar — 25, 26, 31
- Nepal — 26, 36, 37
- North Korea — 26, 31
- Oman — 26, 35
- Pakistan — 29, 33, 39
- Palestine — 26
- Philippines — 26, 74
- Qatar — 26
- Saudi Arabia — 26, 34-35, 39
- Singapore — 25, 26, 27, 53
- South Korea — 25, 27
- Sri Lanka — 24, 27
- Syria — 27, 64
- Tajikistan — 27
- Thailand — 25, 27
- Timor-Leste — 27, 71
- Turkmenistan — 27, 39
- United Arab Emirates — 27
- Uzbekistan — 27, 39
- Vietnam — 24, 27, 31
- Yemen — 27

THE AMERICAS

- Antigua and Barbuda — 40, 52
- Argentina — 20, 40, 52
- The Bahamas — 40
- Barbados — 40, 41
- Belize — 40, 75
- Bolivia — 40, 48-49, 52
- Brazil — 40, 44-45
- Canada — 40, 46-47
- Chile — 40, 49
- Colombia — 24, 41, 49
- Costa Rica — 41
- Cuba — 41
- Dominica — 7, 25, 38, 41, 50-51
- Dominican Republic — 41
- Ecuador — 7, 25, 38, 41, 50-51
- El Salvador — 41, 51
- Grenada — 25, 41
- Guatemala — 41, 64
- Guyana — 40, 45
- Haiti — 40
- Honduras — 25, 40, 41
- Jamaica — 38, 40, 51
- Mexico — 40, 41, 43, 64
- Nicaragua — 40, 41, 51
- Panama — 40, 41
- Paraguay — 40, 74
- Peru — 40, 49, 65
- Saint Kitts and Nevis — 41, 51
- Saint Lucia — 41
- Saint Vincent and the Grenadines — 40, 41
- Suriname — 41, 51
- Trinidad and Tobago — 41
- United States of America — 41, 42-43, 66
- Uruguay — 40, 41, 52
- Venezuela — 41, 65

AFRICA

- Algeria — 39
- Angola — 54
- Benin — 54
- Botswana — 54, 75
- Burkina Faso — 54, 55
- Burundi — 54
- Cameroon — 54, 57
- Cape Verde — 54
- Central African Republic — 54
- Chad — 54
- Comoros — 39, 54
- Côte d'Ivoire — 24, 55
- Democratic Republic of the Congo — 54, 55
- Djibouti — 54
- Egypt — 8, 55, 64
- Equatorial Guinea — 55
- Eritrea — 55
- Eswatini — 10, 23, 55, 59
- Ethiopia — 54, 55, 56-57, 60
- Gabon — 55
- Gambia — 54, 55
- Ghana — 55, 60
- Guinea — 55, 57
- Guinea-Bissau — 55
- Kenya — 55, 58, 59
- Lesotho — 55, 63
- Liberia — 53
- Libya — 35, 39, 54
- Madagascar — 54
- Malawi — 53, 54
- Mali — 54
- Mauritania — 39, 54
- Mauritius — 54
- Morocco — 54
- Mozambique — 54
- Namibia — 54, 55, 61
- Niger — 24, 54
- Nigeria — 54
- Republic of the Congo — 54, 55
- Rwanda — 54
- São Tomé and Príncipe — 55
- Senegal — 55
- Seychelles — 55
- Sierra Leone — 55
- Somalia — 55, 61
- South Africa — 55, 62, 63
- South Sudan — 55
- Sudan — 55
- Tanzania — 55
- Togo — 55, 61
- Tunisia — 39, 55
- Uganda — 55, 64
- Zambia — 55
- Zimbabwe — 55

OCEANIA

- Australia — 66, 68
- Fiji — 66, 67
- Kiribati — 66, 67
- Marshall Islands — 66
- Micronesia — 66, 67
- Nauru — 66, 67
- New Zealand — 66, 68-69
- Palau — 53, 66, 73
- Papua New Guinea — 66, 70-71
- Samoa — 66
- Solomon Islands — 25, 64
- Tonga — 38, 66
- Tuvalu — 66, 67
- Vanuatu — 66, 72-73

GLOSSARY

The **AGE OF SAIL** refers to a period in maritime history during which sailing ships dominated global sea travel, exploration, trade and naval warfare.

The **BRITISH EMPIRE** was a global empire that, at its height in the late 19th and early 20th centuries, occupied territories on every inhabited continent. The empire began to decline after World War II, leading to a wave of independence movements that resulted in the decolonisation of many countries by the mid-20th century.

COATS OF ARMS are unique designs which are used as symbols of countries, monarchs, regions and even families.

COLONIALISM is a system in which one country takes control of another territory, often by settling its own people there and exploiting the land's resources.

COMMUNISM is an idea about how to run a country where everyone shares everything equally, meaning that all property and resources belong to the community or the government instead of individuals.

DECOLONISATION is the process through which countries that were once controlled by colonial powers gain independence and become self-governing.

EMBLEM is a symbol or design that represents a particular idea, organisation or group.

IDEOLOGY is a set of beliefs, values and ideas that shapes the way individuals or groups understand the world and their place in it.

INDEPENDENCE for a country means that it becomes free from the control of another country and can make its own rules and decisions.

INDIGENOUS refers to the original people who have lived somewhere for a long time and have their own unique cultures, languages and traditions that are connected to that land.

The **MIDDLE AGES** was a period in European history from around the 5th to the late 15th century, shaping much of Europe's culture, society and politics.

A **MONARCHY** is a system of government where a single person, called a king or queen, rules a country, usually for life and often passed down through family lines.

A **NATIONAL ANTHEM** is a formal song that represents a country, often expressing its values, history and pride, and is typically played during official events and ceremonies.

PAN-AFRICAN refers to a movement and ideology that seeks to promote unity, solidarity and cooperation among all people of African descent.

PAN-ARAB refers to a movement and ideology that seeks to promote unity, solidarity and cooperation of Arab countries and people.

A **PENNANT** is a long, narrow flag that tapers to a point or has a triangular shape.

A **REPUBLIC** is a type of government where people elect their leaders to represent them.

SOCIALISM is a system where the government owns and shares resources with the idea that everyone has access to basic needs.

The **SOVIET UNION** or USSR was a large communist state in Eastern Europe and Northern Asia that existed from 1922 to 1991, made up of multiple republics, including Russia.

The **SPANISH EMPIRE** was one of the first global empires, stretching across the Americas, parts of Europe, Africa and Asia from the late 15th century to the early 19th century.

STATE HERALD is an official that manages and designs symbols like coats of arms, flags and emblems.

TREASURY is a government department or institution responsible for managing a country's finances.

VEXILLOIDS are objects that resemble flags but are not actual flags, such as poles, banners or emblems. They were often used in ceremonial contexts before the development of modern flags.

VEXILLOLOGIST is a person who studies flags, their history, design, symbolism and usage.